The Space Shuttle

Focus: Information

PETER SLOAN &
SHERYL SLOAN

This is a
space shuttle.

The space shuttle
blasts off.

The space shuttle
travels into space.

The astronaut works
in the space shuttle.

The astronaut
works in space.

The space shuttle
comes home.

The astronauts
leave the
space shuttle.